D1711529

A Moment of Violence

War Poetry by Luke Ryan

Dedicated to the Ranger family

Foreword by the author

This will be my second book of war poetry. My experiences with war and violence are broad – several events as a child growing up overseas, my time in the military, and some trips into conflict areas since – but I will admit they are short. I did not serve for 20+ years in the military, and I do not have the breadth of experience that, say, a Ranger with a dozen deployments to Afghanistan might have. I certainly don't have the kind of experience a WWII paratrooper or Vietnam-era infantryman might have.

However, in writing *The Gun and the Scythe*, I found that there are still an infinite number of corners to explore in the subject of physical conflict. This is true with any part of the human experience, war only being one of them (and yet, inextricably tied into all the rest). For every idea that surfaces in a place of violence, hundreds of other ideas could be unpacked.

As I have continued to write war poetry, I have been attempting to unpack more ideas from different angles. I have found the process therapeutic and often unpredictable – you don't really know what's lurking in your own mind, especially when it comes to events like a firefight or a funeral.

For every topic under the sun, I am convinced you could write a dozen books of poetry. Here is a meager attempt at one.

1

Boy

A boy sits in the corner
Surrounded by men
In suit jackets and ties
Immersed in a pool of white hair and tiny wrinkles
around the eyes.

His shirt is a bit too big
His tie is a bit too small
His hands are clasped together
He sits still as the others discuss matters of "great
importance."

Their voices carry age
Years bent over the keyboard
And years bent toward the dollar
Like parched men clamoring for a mirage.

But they are young, and the boy is old.
The boy remembers wiping blood off his trousers.
He remembers clearing a malfunction out of his rifle
And firing it back at live men, only one year ago.

He remembers pressing as hard as he could
Trying to hold the life in a wounded man
When the life threatened to pour out of him,
Like a finger in the dam of all things that matter.

He remembers these things as he sits quietly in the
corner.
"Get some coffee," one says.
"Alright." The boy stands;
He pours quietly, stirs quietly, and hands it off.

Quiet Remembrances in Quiet America

If you drive into a small American town
You'll probably find it:
A pillar or a headstone,
A plaque or a statue.
Some remembrance of those who departed on their
country's behalf
And never found their way home.

They can be counted in every small corner
Of every state
Well maintained through every season
By every generation.

You may know of the great monuments to the east
Grand statues you travel great distances to see.
But what of the quiet remembrances?
Built by hometown friends and brokenhearted
parents;
Built by the sons and daughters of American blood,
Just around the corner and down the street.

A Piece of Metal

Medal of metal
What are you for?
You are sterile and cold.
You shine in the eyes of others,
But you do not shine in mine.

Physical Therapy

After the race is run
You may walk,
You may smile,
But do not stop.

Find another race if you must,
Walk for the sake of walking,
Or run for the sake of running,
But do not stop.

For if you stop,
You will begin to fall apart,
Your limbs and your joints
Will disintegrate like wet paper.

For our bodies are held up by forward momentum.
The proof is in the dead,
Those who stopped.
By their own choice,
Or by the choice of the wind.

Stillness and Movement

The movement of the body is fueled by the stillness
of the heart.
The stillness of the heart is fueled by the stillness of
the body.
And so, the movement of the body is fueled by the
stillness of itself.

Tattoo

I got my first tattoo
And with it a concerned remark:
"Won't you grow tired
Of the same mark in the same spot
Year after year?"

I may have agreed with them once
Until I was made acutely aware
Of the temporary nature of skin
And everything underneath it.

I got my tattoos
Because I liked them,
But even if I didn't
I won't have them for long.

Legionnaires

A legionnaire sat in a field of corpses
Each clutching toward the sky
Like a field of unholy flowers
Grasping for sunlight.

His sword lay across his lap.
Sweat and dirt united into mud,
Smearing into the blood that was spattered onto his
armor
Which shone no more.

His work was finished.
He had swum through the ocean of metal and meat,
And he emerged with little more than scrapes and
bruises.
It was time to rest, just for a moment.
Time to rest and look.

Thoughts swam through this tired man's head.
They were private thoughts,
Though even if he wanted to speak them
He would not know which words to choose.

As the wars rolled onward
Like avalanches of flame, rolling through history,
The legionnaire would come to know
The eternal group he joined that day.

He would come to know
That the warrior a thousand years before
And a thousand years ahead
Would sit on the same fields with the same thoughts,
And that he is one of many.

A Smile in the Grim

One might miss the smirk in the middle of the night
Because it was too dark to see.
But the smirk was there nonetheless.

"Doom and gloom, doom and gloom!"
"It's a curse, it's an unbearable burden!"
There are veins of truth here, I suppose.

But it was not all doom and gloom
We laughed among the ruins
We played games when others thought we ought to
cry.

Not every moment was one of reverence.
All this talk of brotherhood and the blood spilled
among it,
Yet we forget that laughter was a primary ingredient
of it all.

Hurry Up and Wait

Lines to paper
Lines to pouches
Lines to pilfer
The parcels.

Lines to water
Lines to wait
Lines to weather
The worst of the war.

Lines to laze
Lines to lase
Lines to line up
Behind lines of lines.

Agency

My choices are like the strokes of an oar.
The ocean tosses my boat from wave to wave,
The wind takes me where it pleases.

I can see when the power of the water exceeds the
power of my arms,
But the strokes of my oars are my own,
The fruits of my exertion belong to me.

I am who I describe myself to be.
I am a book that I have written,
A statue I have sculpted,
A child I have raised.

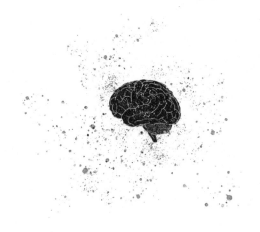

Such Little Time for Such Grand Things

It was there that my body failed.
It had never failed before,
I had built it with iron and stone.
I was strong, and known by my peers as strong—

And yet
Comparing the strength of bodies on the battlefield
Is like comparing the strength of paper houses
In the middle of a furnace.

I lay in the fields
I lay in the rocks
I lay in the sky
I lay and my breath escapes my lips.

I long for the touch of some stranger
As I clutch the fabric of my own clothing
In the dirt of a country
Far away.
So far away.

The sun sears the sky,
Dirt is in the cracks of my skin
In my mouth
There's blood on my shirt.
I don't know who it belongs to.

Will I die in this place?
There are images that shuffle through my mind
They seem like memories
But I don't know who they belong to.

Images of a woman, beautiful and kind.
Her skin is soft, and her heart is softer—
A child, an infant, in my arms,
A daughter in a field bathed in sunlight,
A son smiling and waving at—
Is it me? Or someone beyond me?

Two hands clasped together,
Hands with wrinkles and veins
The distant sound of laughter
Fading like a ghost in the fog.

I don't want to die in this place.
Are those memories my own?
Please let them be mine.

I look to the man next to me.
He has also been adorned with blood,
And I know that it is his.
He is my kin,
Though our parents have never met.

No, please let these memories be his.
Yes, better his than mine.

Such time we have.
Such little time for such grand things.

A Raw Wound

Often times a wound will close.
The clock places its healing hands upon it,
And though the scars remain,
The doors of pain have closed.

Others are not so simple.
Others are permanently rubbed raw.
The clock still works its healing hands,
But a part is always skinned.

The crude laceration can be forgotten
Until another is added to the pile.
Each addition is a new reminder
Of the first begotten wound.

Stop

Stop the circus
Stop the lights
Freeze the traffic
Stay the sirens.

One breath,
A single mind,
A living mind,
Living now.

Living in the moment between seconds,
The moment crisp air hits the skin,
The moment a winged creature turns its head,
The moment of silence between words and whispers.

The Rising Glow

What are the fruits of my labor?
Did the movement of my hands once subvert the
rivers of history?
Or were they just clatter and clamor,
Chaotic movement among storming oceans?

The great flames of my life—
Now living in some distant past,
Are they now little more than embers, shedding their
last tears of light?
Are they no more than ashes rising into an overcast
sky?

And yet
Perhaps the flames were never found in the inferno,
For those who have journeyed in
Know the great blaze ignited by a small match.

Blessed am I, to be caught in these small moments
every day.

May the flames be stoked once again
In a word of kindness,
A hand to the downtrodden,
And a breath of color to the ashen.

Thank You For Your Service

I saw an elderly woman standing in the street
As I drove by in my air-conditioned vehicle.
Her days of labor ought to be behind her,
And yet there she stood,
A sign in her hand and a vest on her back.
She waved across throngs of children,
And stood between them and oncoming vehicles.

What had I done that day?
What had I offered those around me?
How had I served anyone but myself
On that day I spent in the air-conditioning?

We are all cogs in a great machine
The family, the nation, the human race.
Countless serve to the betterment of the other,
And countless more do not.

And on that day
That woman served
And I did not.

The Tired Call

I can feel a sickness
It grows year after year,
Call after call.
A name on my phone and a lump in my throat.

It's a pit in the stomach;
A sickness made of grief,
And a deep, deep fatigue
As old as war itself,
But as new as the morning mist.

Tired, is the only word I know for it.
Very tired.
Simple words
For a simple feeling.

"We lost him, man.
It was another fight,
In another place,
And now he's gone."

"He couldn't do it anymore,
That tired sickness,
It crept and fueled the fire of every other crack and
crevice in his life.
He left on his own terms,
But not on ours."

"I don't know what's going to happen,
But he got torn up and torn up bad,
And as such our hearts are torn.
We'll help how we can, for they would do the same."

"I'll keep you posted."
"I'll keep you posted."
"I'll keep you posted."

Fully realizing that I was one of the lucky ones,
And doubly blessed to have known such a family.

I let the weight rest on my shoulders.
It's okay if it sits there for a while.
I twist my head and look the burden in its dark,
melancholy eyes;
I give it a nod and say as I always do:
It's okay to be a bit tired.

Anthem for Doomed Elderly

And what of the elderly?
Whose funerals passed so long ago.
Left with distant guns that have melted into the sand,
Left to listen to prayers and bells.
They can hear the choirs mourn
Once a passing year,
A gracious and elegant reminder
Of the demented choirs passed.

Shall they light a candle for the doomed youth?
With hands of leather and eyes of old,
Should they let the fallen remain in the dark?
Would it mock them to light a candle and join a choir?
The pallor of the girls' brows has passed;
Their flowers are scattered among the winds of time.

This Too Shall Pass

We are shivering in a midnight downpour,
Shaking and striking a flint onto wet wood.
Sparks are flung into existence
And snuffed out at the sound of torrential tribulation.

My thoughts are frantic,
Scattered with my dying sparks.
I think not of the coming morning.
I think not of the sun that will rise and the sky that
will appear between the clouds.

But the sun always comes,
As sure as the evening it comes.
And yet only I can choose
Where my mind shall linger.

LIFE

We saw three infant kittens
Shivering in the rain
Huddled among one another,
Each little piles of gentle fur
Inhaling misery and exhaling despair.
They were thrown into the thorns of mother earth,
As cruel and indifferent as she is beautiful.

We picked them up and brought them home,
It wasn't long before the first one perished—
Never given a breath of joy or the gift of warmth,
though at least he found rest.
The others clung to life like a starving man on a piece
of driftwood,
Except they were born in the ocean,
Tossed about by the waves since the day they first
drew breath above the surface.

Tender things birthed onto concrete,
And yet they grew.
What a blessing to see a small, shivering thing eat.
What a blessing to see it do all the things you turn
your nose up at,
For if you can turn your nose up at the actions of a
thing,

Then that thing must be living,
And few things are more precious than the smallest
lives.

To take life is easy.
A small movement as a finger pulls the trigger,
A small push of the knife or shove of the shoulder.
We are fragile beasts, snatched into oblivion with a
thought and a twitch.
So tediously we balance on the knife-blade of breath
and flesh.

To bring life is hard.
To sit on the bathroom floor with food in your hand
For untold hours and untold days
As sick things take tiny morsels from your palm,
Gaining strength in such minor increments,
Reminding one that a marathon is composed of
countless, gentle steps.

Then one evening
You see those small, precious things
Curled up on the couch,
Bodies full and muscles strong.
Eyes tight in cherished warmth:
The warmth of life, of comfort, of ease, and the
warmth of one another.
And then you feel the warmth of life—
A gift from hardship.

This is the warmth.
This is the soul at its rarest bloom.

A Path at Nightfall

The world is stripped to black
On the path at nightfall.
The skyscrapers and the mountains alike
Fall into obscurity,
Like shadows in the dark.

There is only the strip of dirt ahead
And the light that bleeds onto it.

The Quatrain of Battle

Move—
All as one, a single creature intent on havoc.
Shoot—
Loose the lightning, fling forth the thunder.
Communicate—
For the fingers are an extension of a mind that speaks
to its body.
Kill—
Times are short, and at times they must be shorter.

The Killing

A life taken
That is the act
Killing
That is the word.

No feelings of twisted confusion
Nor feelings of icy nothingness
Are more than the action itself,
That act of killing.

The action is what deserves the time in the light,
As does he who was taken.
Not the taker,
For we still have the gift of breath.

Do not shy away from what the thing is,
Lest the thing become some web,
Departed from its definition.
Departed from the reality,
Departed from the killing.

Do Not Shy Away

This is the truth,
Truth in the raw.
It ought to make your stomach turn,
It ought to make mind grow hot with rage.

Knowledge is a heavy weight,
It must be carried by all,
It must be known by all,
Lest it fall into oblivion.

Mindfulness Now

Is my head crawling in the mud?
Or is the mud crawling in my head?
A dash of ice-cold water and a slap of clarity,
I must draw myself from the battles long gone,
And immerse myself in the second,
Ticking through the same air that fills my lungs.

We live in a series of moments,
Moments that pass like the flight of a bullet.
But our minds live in an ocean of moments,
Moments passed and moments to come.

Would that we live in the second as it passes.
Would that we admire the warmth on our skin,
Instead of comparing it to the cold of the past
Or the heat of the future.

Prayer

"If one is wounded,
Let it be me.
If one is killed,
Let it be me."

This was my prayer
This was their prayer.
My prayer was not answered.
Their prayers were answered.

The Statue of Men

No justice can be had
When one strikes his fingers to the keys
And writes about the human experience.

Surely then, no justice can be had
When one attempts to describe the indescribable—
The birth of a child or the death of the same.

Or perhaps a little justice can be had
A piece of it, like a tiny, shining pearl
Carried by a speaker to a great silhouette of our
understanding.

On its own, that pearl would be swallowed whole,
A useless thing with no frame to stand upon.
But in the company of pearls, each with their own
vibrance
They build a statue.

The statue resembles that of a human being,
Though it does not have limbs.
It is a statue of the human heart,
Its inclinations,
Its long history of gentle kisses,
And its long history of bloody swords.

Many will take a pearl from the shelf.
Some study it, others simply marvel at its shine;
All must be found.

Did You Forget?

"To serve"—
What did that mean to you?
What value does that coin hold
If you cast it aside now?

Will you ask for others to bend to you
Because in your youth you bent to them?
That is not a service,
That is an exchanging of services.
An economy of favors.

Why do you shrug off the cloak
That you look so fondly upon?

21 Rounds

1. The day you opened your eyes; you cried, and I wept.
2. You pieced together words like the plastic shapes on the carpet.
3. The first time you handed Mister Bear to your sister.
4. The number of times you fell off your tricycle, and the number of times you got back up again.
5. You stepped into a classroom, out of sight but always in mind.
6. The number of figures in the drawing that still hangs on my refrigerator.
7. Big teeth pushed the little ones out.
8. Grandpa visited every day, and you sat on his knee as he whispered about his youth in turmoil and shadow. Your eyes widened at the thought of a life with weight.
9. You and your friends charging through the woods with toy guns and paper flags.
10. The number of stitches in your arm when you crashed right through the window overlooking the porch.
11. Sitting on the living room floor, plastered to the television and watching every action hero as they braved flames and hurricanes.

12. The number of eggs you dropped in the middle of the kitchen floor. I yelled but I wished that I had laughed.

13. We waved to Grandpa as he was lowered into the earth. You held my hand and we both wept.

14. Your first kiss. You didn't think I knew, but I knew.

15. The number of times you were grounded for sneaking out of the house that year.

16. When I caught you drinking. I didn't mind that you did, just that you lied.

17. You hugged me and told me you were glad for everything I've done.

18. The day you walked up the stage and the day you left to futures untold.

19. The moment you raised your right hand.

20. When you boarded a plane and went to a faraway place.

21. The number of rounds they fired when we returned you to the earth. I cried, and you slept.

Clinging

Some memories cling to the mind
Like sand in a bed.
And some minds cling to the memories,
Addicted to reliving a few moments of meaning.
As sensible as bringing a bed to the beach.

A Girl at Arlington

Where there is death
There is undeniable life.
For every tree that decays
Another grows in its place.

Tears of grief fall in one room
While tears of joy in another.
As a soldier is lowered into his resting place at
Arlington
So a girl treads among its headstones.

This is not the battle of light and dark,
And these are not two sides to some coin.
It is a dance of life and a dance of death,
Forever interwoven among one another.

Embrace them both,
And you will relish the prior.
Embrace them both,
And you will not fear the latter.

Undiscovered Country

You explored fields of shredded flags and broken
flesh.
You explored the heart of Cain and the loss of Abel.
You explored the last moments of the martyrs
And the defining moments of the damned.

To where will you depart now?
All you who have returned home.
Some will find a comfortable chair
And sink into it, like madman into a padded cell.
Explorers no more.

Others will hoist the sails once again
And depart into the waters of their own souls.
For it is vast, undiscovered country.
Their ships, cracked and weathered,
Are stronger for their past voyages.
They point their compasses inward
And explore once again.

Nothing is Heavier Than Nothing At All

Light is strength
Darkness is nothing
Strike a match
Darkness dies.

What To Do With What Has Been Bought

There were four men
Whose hearts lived among the freedom of ocean
waves,
But whose bodies lay in the desert.
And so, they set out together toward the coast.

The first gathered water in jugs.
He carried them and supplied water to the rest.
By the time the sand turned to grass
He fell to the earth, his eyes shut, and his soul
departed,
For he had given all his water to the others.

They came upon a cliff, and they could hear the
waves on the other side.
The second man hoisted them up,
But their rope was frayed and torn.
As he elevated the second, he knew it would not last
another.
He hoisted them up anyway, remaining behind,
Listening to the waves, just out of reach.

As their feet hit the sand,
The third man picked up saw, hammer, and nail
And he toiled beneath the sun
Until his muscles gave out
And his eyes turned to glass.
Before his body and among the seashells lay a great boat,
Its wood and sails in perfect condition,
With only one last man to sail it.

The last man stood with a smile on his face
And let the ocean kiss his toes.
He looked at the boat
And smiled again,
But his face soon twisted and turned
For he did not know how to sail.
His father had taught him as a boy,
But he had forgotten, and it would surely be too dangerous to try.
He hung his head
And mumbled that perhaps the beach was good enough.

Shrouded in Midnight

Side by side we sat
In the belly of a bird
Made of steel parts and iron men
Who had cut their teeth on blood long ago.

We flew together
Heading to a wretched place
Where wretched men
Hid among beautiful and timeworn mountains.

Our futures were shrouded in midnight,
And we did not know the path that lay before us.

Would we step into the Afghan dirt and tread through
tilled up farmlands?
Would it be a quiet night as we crept into the home of
our enemy
And caught him before he woke?
Would he exit with hands raised and eyes lowered?
Or would we find little more than an empty room and
a broken motorcycle?

Our futures were shrouded in midnight,
And we did not know the path that lay before us.

Would we stumble upon a viler undertaking?
Would we find prisoners or stacks of rifles?
Would we enter a room that smelled of diesel?
And that sinister combination of fertilizer?

Our futures were shrouded in midnight,
And we did not know the path that lay before us.

Or perhaps we would be greeted with an eruption of
gunfire,
The flash of a muzzle or the heat of an explosion.
Perhaps in a matter of minutes we would see the
blood of our brothers
Spilled among the blood of a shooter,
Who died with malice on his lips.

We sat together on that bird of steel,
Under the stars and over the mountains.
The minutes dwindled down and the wheels touched
the dirt,
And we placed our boots onto Afghan soil.

Whatever fate that midnight held,
We knew that we would meet it together
And that was enough for us.

Cheers

Cheers to sons of fallen soldiers
Cheers to the daughters who never were
Cheers to the generations of unknown faces
Those who may have saved the world.

Cheers to the families of vacant spaces
Cheers to the sunsets to pass unseen
Cheers to deeds undone by combat
And above all,
Cheers to the lives confined to memory.

The Eternal Present

What can I keep?
The gold in my hands turns to dust,
My memories turn to smoke,
And my home turns to ash.

I can keep the present moment
A precious, single thing.
It stretches into the furthest reaches of eternity,
And evaporates the instant it is born.

We dance always,
Bound to one another,
Our fingers woven together,
The present and I.

These eternal moments
Are fused together into an eternal one,
As quick as thunder
And as old as the sun.

That eternal present is where I live.
Where soft skin is a miracle,
Where good whiskey feeds the soul,
And where a short embrace lasts a lifetime.

Shots Fired in Anger

I was a boy of ten
When I first heard shots fired in anger
Echoing through the bazaar,
Bouncing off the wood and glass and bread.

"One man killed another," my father said,
"Shot him dead in the street."
"Why?"
"One believed in one thing, the other another.
They had words and their hands were violent,
And one was taken from the main."

What a foolish act, I thought.
To murder a man over conflicting beliefs.
Is that not a savage thing?
Would civilized men not choose discourse over
violence if given the chance?
Could they not put their weapons on their hips and
use their words?
Would they not jerk away from the entangling vines
of blood and violence?

What a silly thing,
For two systems of belief
To be so embroiled in rage.
To insist that there must be two distinct sides,
In every word and every act,
That one is always a right pillar and the other always
the bastion of evil.
As if this were not a complicated world.

If that is true, that civilized men and women act in
greater ways,
Then civilization is a myth,
In every country,
All the time.

How to Make a Human Inhuman

Step one:
That man is a purveyor of terrible deeds,
How could one step in a line so crooked as his?

Step two:
A supporter of the man means they are a supporter of the act,
Are not all supporters of the act guilty all the same?

Step three:
Supporters of the act might as well have carried it out with their own hands,
And who could see such malice through?

Step four:
Only a purveyor of terrible deeds, a thing devoid of conscience and poise.
Only a creature is devoid of such humanity.

Step five:
All those who share that crooked line must be cut of the same cloth.
Creatures all, one and the same.

Animals.
One and the same.

Disturbed Earth

The earth here is disturbed
I do not know what lies beneath.
All I know is that pressure will bring pain.

I walk around it
I walk around it
I always walk around it
And I attribute my life to this.

But I must fall to my knees
And unearth the thing that lay below.
Dig, detect, disarm.
Dig, detect, disarm.

Starting Pistol

He waits on the starting block,
His ears burn,
The bumps on his arm stretch forth,
As if they would give him a head start.

In his racing days,
There was always a pistol.
Now there was none,
Yet he waits for one anyway.

One day, he is too old to stand,
So, he takes a seat at the edge of the pool
And wonders to himself aloud,
"Why did no one fire the pistol? I remember they
used to fire the pistol."

Freedom Defined

"Freedom"
A word we know
A word we use
A word we love.

But what gears turn behind that word?
Who were the men who won it?
What exactly did that win?

Freedom is not the image of a young boy running
underneath a waving flag,
Nor is it the sun rising over the plains of the
heartland,
Though these images are radiant within.

Freedom has been mistaken for the feeling of free
men,
For those who recognize true freedom focus not its
symbols,
But on the responsibility it lays at our feet.

A Flight

I stepped onto a plane
And watched the same familiar routine:
The earth shrank away, and the sky turned to an
infinite ocean
On which we were an overturned raft.

Many flights have I taken.

Flying to an island
An island of laughter and lights
An island of bare skin peppered with sand
An island of primal moments.

Flying to labor
The labor of production
The labor of shaking hands
The labor of deficit and gain.

Flying to my home
Home and to those toward which my heart extends
Home to furry legs and a wagging tail
Home to the things burrowed deep.

Flying to war
A war with the things of the island
A war with the things of my labor
A war with the things of my home.

A war in world I know
Connected by the same land I watch fall beneath me,
And yet a world set apart
By countless miles measured by my thoughts.

It Started with a Bang

It started with a bang and ended with a whimper,
It was the first time violence touched my fingertips.
I was a child in a country filled with those who loved me,
Those who never thought anything special of me,
And those who burst and bubbled in rage at the thought of me.

We hid under desks
As armed men hunted us
We did not cry out
Lest they steal the breath from our lungs.

Helpless worms were we
Stretched out on the pavement,
Praying that we would not be stomped upon,
As others were ushered on to the next world.

Children ought not to suffer such things,
Children ought not to cower and cringe at the hands of violent men.
And yet children we were,
And suffer we did.

It was the first time violence reached out to me with its long and jagged fingers,
A prologue to a long story of the same.

Have You Ever Seen Tanks on Your Street?

Have you ever seen tanks on your street?
A street where familiar houses sit side-by-side,
Each one with its own beaming grin,
And one that you know is the forge of your fondest
memories.

Where children careen around the corners,
Where smiles are packed into the soil,
Where Laughter is watered
And futures grow.

Hearts might have been broken there,
And there have been skinned knees and chipped
teeth,
But tanks on the street—
A reminder of another ancient state of homo sapiens
That we insist has been forgotten.

Tanks on the street.
This street.
My street.
That is something new.

Piles

Piles of memories
Stacked on top of bodies
Stacked on top of friends
Stacked on top of strangers.

Piles of hate
Stacked on top of those dark parts of myself
Stacked on top of my skewed perception of others
Stacked on top of all the wrong ways to look at
things.

Piles of stress
Stacked on top of money
Stacked on top of a bitter word between lovers
Stacked on top of itself, over and over.

Piles love
Staked on top of those memories
Stacked on top of hate
Stacked on top of stress—

Flattening them all
Into a foundation on which we stand
And build piles of laughter,
Stacked on top of piles of years.

The Firing of a Few Guns at Night

A flash and a bang and a flash-flash-flash
A cry and a whimper and the spilling of blood.

Our souls now swim in a lake of gasoline
And matches rain from the sky.

The Sniper

An invisible line pierces the lonely flakes of snow,
A cross on one side and a dead man on the other.
The same line has pierced heavy rain in the jungle,
It has pierced air so dry it would sap the tears from
your face.

It is the line of a long gun,
Behind which lies a man with a long fuse.
He is as still as a corpse buried in rock,
Save for the drop of his breath and the drop of the
hammer.

He lives by a handful of lone virtues:

The Protector
His overwatch spans like wings over his brethren
And he will spit fire at those who would breach those
sacred borders.

The Patient One
He understands the infinite nature of time
And so, he waits, when waiting is what is needed.

The Owning of a Single Moment
When the moment arrives, his entire life is born to it
The second hand ticks to that single sliver in time,
and the primer strikes that single round.

The Thin Veneer

There is a thin veneer
Between us and much of the world.
A curtain of light and lust,
A curtain of motion and frenzy.

Behind that curtain lay the majority.
We push our periscopes through,
We point with tearful eyes, shutting it off (for we
cannot bear any more),
And at best we turn and apply their lessons to
ourselves.
Or pretend we are no different,
Pointing what appears to be a humble finger inward,
But diminishing the whole thing instead.

The curtain remains,
Like the Great Wall, it remains steadfast.
Few tread past its borders.
Fewer still choose life on the other side.
And fewer seek to tear the whole curtain down.

The Smells of War

The lubricant of weapons—
The grease that cycles the iron that catapults lead.

The dirt of the east—
That grit compacted into fabric and skin.

The cold sweat, matted from the night—
A night freezing in air, sweltering in movement.

They say smell lasts the longest,
But I can't remember them
Until the scent is reintroduced.
Reintroduce the sound of gunfire
And I think I would remember that too.

The Pen and the Brush

Those who have been given a pen
Have been given a directive:
Write what you know,
Write who you know,
Write how you know.

It's a treacherous business,
Like painting a mountain and claiming its truth.
Those who live on the far side of the mountain will
cry out in protest,
For they see a different rock.
At times the mountain on the page appears a little too
short,
Or the color of the sky a little too blue,
A missed mark mistaken for a moment of malice,
Followed by cries of protest.

Still,
The mountain is more than an assortment of rocks
and trees,
It's a mountain of virtue, memory, and beauty in the
rough.
Such things must be painted with the pen and the
brush.

Hats and Feathers

I want to fill my hat with feathers
To adorn it with green and blue
And all the shimmering colors
Of all the mythical birds.

Feathers of metal
Feathers of cloth
Feather of duty and hardship
Feathers of all my exaggerated tales.

And yet I fill my hat with bricks
My friends will watch me as I fly
Down to the bottom of the ocean.

Dreams of a Violent Past

There are dreams, there are nightmares,
And then there is scar tissue
Revealing its ugly face
As my eyes close and my thoughts drift into memory.

At night, my thoughts do as they please
And I am at the mercy of the wind.

Can these dreams be woven out?
Can I rip the threads from their roots
And burn them in my bare hands?

If the answer is no,
Then I dread every tired night ahead.

And if the answer is yes,
Would I even want them gone?

A Son Called to War

Oh, my son.
While the countless voices bicker among one another,
A voice called out, asking you to tread among the
flames,
And you have answered, my dear child.

I too have trodden among those flames,
Years ago, when I was young.
We were all so young.

But fighting is easy for men like us,
It stretches and wears at the soul,
But it's easy because the way is clear.

Oh, my son.
I thought I had skin in the game then.
I was wrong.

Rest

A great storm stirs within me.
Its clouds are made of ancient stone
And its lightning is slow and unrelenting.
It moves across my heart and it claws at my soul,
And it has long since drained me of tears.

But a fleeting thought—a silent vision,
Drifts across a jagged corner of my mind.
A thought of you.

Of the brooding fire hidden in your eyes.
Of the quiet stream of delicate lines that form your
neck.
Of lips so soft, my tears would return at the touch of
a kiss.

And for that moment, the storm is away.
And for that moment, I rise into the sky and rest.
Glorious rest in the arms of my love.

Made in the USA
Monee, IL
16 June 2020

33724491R00049